DELICIOUS CARIBBEAN RECIPES

Simple, Tasty, Quick, and Easy Meals
From The Caribbean Islands

CLAUDIA CHANCE

Published by Strategic Secrets
www.StrategicSecrets.com
Printed in the United States of America

ISBN-13: 978-1-79202-402-3

CONTENTS

Also published by Strategic Secrets:
Win Now!
Monetize Your Skills
Prayers That Move Heaven
The Certainty of God's Promises
Power-Packed Spiritual Affirmations
Transition to Civilian Life With Confidence

Get these great books and life-changing courses at
www.StrategicSecrets.com.

ACKNOWLEDGEMENTS

I thank God for His blessings on my life and for this opportunity to share this cookbook with you. It is my greatest desire that you enjoy it and share the delicious recipes with your friends, family, and neighbors. Tell everyone about these creative tasty dishes from the Caribbean Islands.

Also, know that whatever you are going through, don't give up. God can make the impossible possible because there's nothing too difficult for Him. Taste and see that the LORD is good. You'll be blessed if you trust in Him. (Psalm 34:8)

I also want to thank my mom who taught me how to cook and bake. She's an inspiration in my life. Her tasty cooking has inspired me to write these delicious Caribbean recipes for you.

FRUITCAKE

Ingredients:

2 lbs. raisins
1/2 lb. mixed peel
1lb. currents
1/2 lb. brown sugar
1/2 lb. prunes
1 cup rum
1/2 lb. cherries
1 lb. butter
1 tsp. salt
1 tsp. spice
1 tsp. nutmeg
1 tsp. vanilla essence
1 tsp. almond essence
1 lb. flour
10 eggs
1 cup black wine or port wine
1 tsp. baking powder
1 cup food coloring

Preparation:

Mince the fruits and soak in 1 cup rum, spices, essence, and wine. Mix these ingredients well and put them into a glass bottle or a jar. Cover and allow mixture to steep for three weeks or longer. When ready to bake the cake, cream butter and sugar in a bowl and mix with a mixer. Add eggs and mix in one by one. Add fruit mixture and stir in 1/2 cup browned sugar coloring to make the mixture light brown in color. Add flour, baking powder and salt. Stir and pour mixture in a greased baking pan. Bake in an oven at 350 degrees for 1 or 2 hours or until done. Pour rum and wine on top after baking. Leave cake in the pan for 3days.

CORN BREAD

Ingredients:

1 cup flour, sifted
1/2 cup sugar
1 cup corn meal
2 eggs
1 cup milk
2 tsps. baking powder
1/2 cup shortening or oil
Pinch of salt
1 cup boiling water

Preparation:

Mix cornmeal, flour, sugar, baking powder and salt in a large bowl. Add melted shortening or oil to mixture. Separate eggs. Beat whites stiff. Beat yolks until lemon color. Pour egg whites in yolks and set aside. Pour hot water in cornmeal mixture, add eggs, and mix lightly. Pour into a greased baking pan and bake in an oven at 350 degrees for 30 minutes.

CASSAVA PONE

Ingredients:

3 cups dry cassava flour
1/2 cup shortening
1 egg
1 1/4 cups sugar
3 cups milk and water
1/2 tsp. orange peel powder
1 tsp vanilla essence
1 tsp. salt
1 1/2 tsps. mixed spice

Preparation:

Grate cassava, wring out the juice, and mix the husk with dry ingredients together in a bowl. Add melted shortening, milk, essence and beaten egg. Blend mixture and pour into a greased shallow pan. Glaze with sugar and water before baking in an oven at 350 degrees for 1 1/2 hours. When grated cassava is used decrease the amount of liquid.

STEAMED CALLALOO

Ingredients:

1lb. fresh Callaloo chopped
1 medium onion chopped
1 tbsp. olive oil
1/4 cup coconut milk
1 tsp. Lawry's seasoning salt
1/4 cup water
1 small tomato chopped
2 cloves garlic chopped

Preparation:

Wash Callaloo thoroughly, cut off the lower end of stems. Chop or cut into strips. In a skillet, fry onions and garlic in olive oil. Add water, Callaloo, coconut milk and seasoning. Cover and steam until almost tender, for 6 minutes. Add chopped tomatoes and steam another few minutes.

CORN PUDDING

Ingredients:

2 cups corn, cooked, kettle or canned
2 cups milk
3 eggs
1 cup onions, finely chopped
1 tbsp. butter, melted
1 tsp. sugar
1/2 cup red sweet peppers, chopped
1 tsp. salt

Preparation:

In a large bowl beat eggs slightly, add all ingredients and mix. Pour mixture into a greased shallow baking pan. Bake in an oven at 350 degrees for 45 minutes or until done.

RICE PUDDING

Ingredients:

2 cups rice cooked
2 tbsps. sugar
1/2 cup raisins
2 cups milk
1 egg
1/2 tsp. nutmeg

Preparation:

In a bowl mix egg, sugar and milk, add other ingredients and stir. Pour into a greased baking pan and bake in an oven at 350 degrees for 40 minutes or until brown.

PLAIN COOKIES

Ingredients:

2 cups flour, sifted
3/4 cup sugar
2/3 cup shortening
1/3 tsp. lemon, grated
1 tsp. vanilla essence
1 egg
4 tbsps. milk
1 1/2 tsps. baking powder
1/4 tsp. salt

Preparation:

In a bowl cream shortening and sugar. Add lemon, vanilla and egg and mix lightly. Add other ingredients and mix. Place dough on a floured surface, roll out and cut into 1/8 inch circles and shape into cookies. Bake in an oven on a greased shallow pan at 375 degrees for 6 or 8 minutes

SPINACH CAKE

Ingredients:

1cup spinach
1 egg
1 cup flour
1 tbsp. onion, finely chopped
1/2 tsp. black pepper
1/2 tsp. salt
2 tbsps. butter
1/2 cup milk
1 cup bread crumbs
1/2 tsp. baking powder

Preparation:

Wash spinach leaves and finely shred with a knife. In a bowl mix egg, add spinach, onions and melted butter. Stir in other ingredients to make a thick batter and shape into cakes with a spoon. Fry in hot oil till golden brown

SHORT PASTRY

Ingredients:

1/2 cup flour, sifted
1 tbsp. butter
3 tsps. shortening
1/2 tsp. sugar
6 tbsps. cold water

Preparation:

Mix flour and butter with a fork in a bowl until mixture looks like bread crumbs. Add water then mix until dough is formed and does not stick to the bowl. On a lightly floured surface roll out dough and cut into desired shapes. Add filling and fold. Bake in an oven at 350 degrees for 30 minutes or until golden brown.

MARBLE CAKE

Ingredients:

1/2 cup flour
2/3 cup sugar
1 cup milk
1 tsp. lime juice
1 1/2 tsps. baking powder
1 1/2 tbsps. cocoa
2 tbsps. butter
2 eggs
1 tsp. vanilla
Red coloring

Preparation:

In a bowl, cream butter and sugar and eggs. Add milk, flour and baking powder and mix well. Divide the mixture into 3 parts. Flavor 1 part with cocoa, 1 with grated lime peel, and the 3rd with vanilla essence and a few drops of coloring. In a greased cake pan pour in alternated spoonfuls of the three mixtures until all is used. Bake in an oven at 350 degrees for 40 minutes or until golden brown

COCONUT SWEET BREAD

Ingredients:

4 cups flour, sifted
1 cup milk
1/2 lb. shortening
1/2 cup sugar
1/2 cup coconut milk
2 1/2 cups grated coconut
2 tsps. vanilla
2 tbsps. baking powder
1 tsp. salt
1 cup raisins
1 egg

Preparation:

Mix sugar, beaten egg, and milk then add melted shortening and vanilla. Add other ingredients and mix. Knead dough lightly on a floured surface. Shape into loaves, put into a greased baking pan, and sprinkle with white sugar. Bake in an oven at 350 degrees for 40 or 50 minutes or until golden brown.

PUNCH A CRÈME

Ingredients:

1 can evaporated milk
3 eggs
1 wine glass of rum
1/2 tsp. lime or orange rind
1 tsp. bitters
1 can condensed milk

Preparation:

In a bowl mix eggs and lime rind well. Add milk, rum and bitters and mix thoroughly. Pour into a bottle, shake well and chill.

BANANA VANILLA ICE CREAM

Ingredients:

4 frozen overripe bananas
2 tsps. vanilla essence
4 tbsps. milk
2 tbsps. almond butter

Preparation:

Peel bananas and cut into chunks. Put bananas into a zip lock bag and freeze. In a food processor blend bananas and almond butter until smooth. Add vanilla and milk, 1 tbsp. at a time, and mix well. Transfer the ice cream into a container, cover and freeze for 20 minutes..

MARBY

Ingredients:

3 ounces Marby bark
2 cups water
2 lbs. sugar
1 tsp. cinnamon
2 tsps. vanilla essence
1 piece orange peel
A few cloves

Preparation:

Wash and boil Marby bark in a pot with water then add cloves, orange peel and cinnamon. Boil for 1/2 hour until very bitter. Strain and mix liquid with water to taste. Add sugar until very sweet, bottle and cover, and leave for three days.

GINGER BEER

Ingredients:

1/2 lb. ginger
1 large lime (green)
2 lbs. sugar (white)
1 gallon water

Preparation:

Scrape ginger, wash and grate. Place in a large bowl, add boiling water and sugar and stir until dissolved. Peel lime, add both lime and rind to the liquid, cool, and pour in a glass bottle or a jar. Let it stand for six days and stir with a wooden spoon each day. When set, strain, pour into bottles and chill..

SORREL BEER

Ingredients:

1/2 lb. sorrel
3 lbs. sugar
1 gallon water (boiling)
1 tsp. cinnamon
1/2 tsp. clove (powder)
1 tsp. spice
1 piece orange peel (dried)
A few cloves

Preparation:

Wash sorrel and boil in a pot with water, orange peel, cinnamon and cloves. Cover and let the liquid steep for two days. Strain the sorrel with a strainer. Let it stand for another two days before serving chilled.

PAWPAW AND MANGO DRINK

Ingredients:

1 cup mango pulp
1 cup pawpaw pulp
1 tsp. grated orange rind
1/4 cup lime juice
4 cups water
1 cup orange juice

Preparation:

Mash mango and pawpaw. Put all ingredients into a blender and blend them. Sugar to taste. Serve chilled.

SOURSOP ICE CREAM

Ingredients:

1 large ripe soursop
2 cups hot water
1/2 can evaporated milk
1 can condensed milk
1 tsp. vanilla essence

Preparation:

Peel and crush soursop in a bowl. Pour in hot water, stir and allow to stand for 1/2 hour. Press the pulp through a large strainer to extract the juice, add vanilla, milk and sugar to taste, freeze and serve.

BAKED EGGPLANT AND CHEESE

Ingredients:

1 large ripe purple eggplant
2 1/2 cups tomato sauce
1 cup cheese, grated
1 tsp. Lawry's seasoning salt

Preparation:

Wash unpeeled eggplant. Cut lengthwise or in round slices. Brush slices lightly with oil and sprinkle with seasoning. Place on a baking sheet and bake for 10 minutes on each sides until tender. Spoon a little tomato sauce into a square or rectangular baking dish and arrange eggplant slices side by side. Cover with tomato sauce and cheese on top. Bake uncovered in an oven at 350 degrees for 15 minutes or until lightly browned.

MACARONI SALAD

Ingredients:

4 cups elbow macaroni
1 cup mayonnaise
3/4 tsp. onion powder
1/4 cup red sweet peppers, diced
1/4 cup onions, finely chopped
1/4 tsp. salt
1/4 cup green peas
6 cups water

Preparation:

Cook macaroni in a pot with boiling water and drain. Pour macaroni into a bowl, add remaining ingredients and stir. Chill and serve.

PLANTAIN LASAGNA

Ingredients:

6 plantains, ripe not soft
1 lb. ground beef
1 28 ounce jar spaghetti sauce
1 tsp. garlic powder
2 cloves garlic, minced
1 tbsp. Lawry's seasoning salt
1 tsp. basil
1 lb. package Monterey cheese
1 tsp. oil
1 tsp. paprika
1/4 cup onions, finely chopped
1/4 cup red sweet peppers, chopped

Preparation:

Peel plantains and slice lengthwise. In a pot with oil simmer onions, peppers and garlic. Add spaghetti sauce, meat and seasonings. Cook for 20 minutes in a greased baking dish. Lay slices of plantains side by side. Add meat mixture on top. Add another layer of plantains and meat. Repeat the layers with the remaining plantains and meat. Sprinkle grated cheese on top. Cover with a piece of foil and bake in an oven at 350 degrees for 40 minutes.

BANANA FRITTERS

Ingredients:

2 ripe bananas
1 tsp. cinnamon
1 cup flour
1 tsp. baking powder
2 tbsps. sugar
1 cup milk
1 tsp. vanilla essence
1/2 tsp. salt
Oil for frying

Preparation:

Mash bananas with a fork in a bowl. Add all ingredients and mix until smooth. Spoon mixture to make small cakes. Fry in shallow oil.

SPINACH SHAKE

Ingredients:

1 cup spinach
1/2 cup bananas (ripe)
3/4 cup strawberries
1 cup milk
1 tbsp. chia seed
1/2 cup ice

Preparation:

Wash spinach. Blend all ingredients in a blender until smooth and serve.

SALT FISH CAKES

Ingredients:

1 lb. salt fish
1 cup flour
1 tsp. onion powder
1 egg
1 tsp. black pepper
1 tbsp. parsley
1 chive, chopped
1/2 tsp lime juice

Preparation:

Soak and boil salt fish to reduce salt. When cool mince salt fish in a bowl. Add all ingredients and mix. Spoon mixture and shape into cakes. Fry in deep or shallow oil.

OATMEAL COOKIES

Ingredients:

1 1/4 cups oats
1 cup flour
1 cup sugar
1/2 cup butter
1 tsp. vanilla essence
1 egg
1/4 cup milk
1 cup raisins
1 tsp. salt
2 tsps. baking powder
A pinch of baking soda

Preparation:

Mix all ingredients in a bowl. Spoon cookie dough and shape into cookies on a greased shallow baking pan. Bake in an oven at 350 degrees for 17 minutes or until golden brown.

PANCAKE OR WAFFLE BATTER

Ingredients:

1 1/2 cups flour
2 tbsps. sugar
1 tsp. baking powder
1/2 tsp. salt
1 tsp. vanilla
2 tbsps. milk

Preparation:

Pour milk and vanilla into a bowl and mix together. Add all other ingredients and mix until smooth. Pour pancake batter into a nonstick frying pan and fry with oil or in a waffle maker follow manufacturer's directions.

KETCHUP

Ingredients:

1 cup tomato puree
1 tbsp. fresh lemon juice
1/2 tsp. onion powder
1 tbsp. oil
1/2 tsp salt
1 tbsp. molasses
1/4 tsp. garlic powder

Preparation:

Blend all ingredients in a blender until smooth.

CALLALOO SOUP

Ingredients:

1 lb. Callaloo
1/2 cup coconut milk
10 cups water
1 cup carrots, sliced
2 cups potatoes, cubed
1/4 cup onions, finely chopped
1/4 cup green sweet peppers, chopped
1 lb. beef
1/2 tsp. black pepper
2 cloves garlic, minced
1 tbsp. Lawry's seasoning salt
1 tsp. tomato paste or ketchup
1 tsp. butter
1 cup flour
4 sprigs fresh thyme

Preparation:

Salt to taste. Wash Callaloo, cut lower stem off and cut into strips. Wash meat, cut into small pieces and add seasoning. In a large pot simmer onions, garlic and pepper with oil. Pour in water and meat. Cook until tender. In a small pot pour in 1/3 cup water and Callaloo. Steam and when cool blend in a blender. Pour into the large pot. Add all ingredients except flour. Make dumplings with the flour, pinch of salt and water. Mix to form a dough. Add dumplings in the pot. Cook for 30 minutes or until done..

BANANA BREAD

Ingredients:

3 ripe bananas, mashed
2 cups flour
1/2 cup butter
1/2 cup sugar
1 egg
1/2 cup nuts, crushed
1/2 cup raisins
1/2 cup milk
3 tsps. baking powder
1 tsp. vanilla essence
1/2 tsp. grated nutmeg
1/2 tsp. salt

Preparation:

Mix sugar, butter and egg with a mixer in a large bowl, until creamy. Add mashed bananas and all other ingredients and mix well. Pour mixture into a greased baking pan and bake in an oven at 350 degrees for 40 minutes or until golden brown.

DOUGHNUTS

Ingredients:

1 package dry yeast
1/4 cup sugar
1/2 cup warm water
2 eggs
1 cup milk
1/2 cup shortening
3 cups flour
1 tsp. salt

Preparation:

In a small bowl mix yeast and sugar in warm water. Let rise for 5 minutes or until bubbly. In a large bowl mix other ingredients, add yeast mixture and stir. Knead on a floured surface and let dough rise for 8 minutes. When dough rises roll out dough 1/2 inch thick, cut dough into doughnut shapes and let rise for 30 minutes until double in size. Shape into doughnut rolls, place in a greased baking pan and bake in an oven at 350 degrees for 20 or 30 minutes. While warm toss doughnuts in white sugar.

BLUE MUFFINS

Ingredients:

1 cup sugar
1 cup milk
1/4 cup oil
1 1/2 cups flour
2 tsps. baking powder
1 tsp. vanilla essence

Preparation:

Mix all ingredients in a bowl, pour into a greased muffin pan and bake in an oven at 350 degrees for 30 minutes.

HOT CROSS BUNS

Ingredients:

1 package dry yeast
1 cup flour
1/4 cup sugar
1/2 tsp. salt
1/4 cup butter
1 cup warm milk
1 tsp. mixed peel
1/2 tsp. spice
1 tsp. ginger, grated

Preparation:

Mix yeast, 2 tsps. sugar with warm milk in a small bowl. Let rise for 5 minutes or until bubbly. In a large bowl mix flour, salt, spice, ginger and sugar, add yeast mixture and other ingredients, mix and knead and let it rise until double in size. Knead once more and shape into buns. Before baking cut to make a cross on the top. Bake in a greased baking pan in an oven at 350 degrees for 30 minutes or until golden brown.

FRUIT PUNCH

Ingredients:

1 banana (ripe)
1 cup orange juice
1/4 cup pineapple, crushed
1 tbsp. lemon juice
1/4 cup apple juice
2 cups ice cubes

Preparation:

In a blender blend ingredients, add ice and blend until smooth. Serve immediately.

PIZZA DOUGH

Ingredients:

1 package dry yeast
2 tbsps. sugar
1 cup warm water
2 1/2 cups flour
1 tsp. salt
1 tbsp. oil

Preparation:

Mix yeast, 2 cups flour and salt in a large bowl. Add warm water, sugar and oil. Mix until smooth then stir in remaining flour to form a stiff dough that pulls away from the sides of the bowl. Place dough on a lightly floured surface, knead for 8 minutes until smooth and elastic and place in oiled bowl. Cover and let rise in a warm place for 30 minutes or until double in size. Divide dough in half and let rise for another 10 minutes. Press each half in 12 inch circle. Sprinkle corn meal in pizza baking pans. Place dough in the pans and bake in an oven at 350 degrees for 20 minutes or until crust begins to brown. Add ingredients for pizza.

PIE CRUST

Ingredients:

2 cups flour
1/2 cup water or milk (cold)
1/4 cup oil
1 tsp. salt

Preparation:

In a bowl mix flour, salt, oil and milk. Form into a ball and divide in half. Roll out each half of dough in large circle. Place in a greased 8 or 9 inch pie pan, add filling and bake in an oven at 350 degrees for 45 minutes or until golden brown.

WHEAT BREAD

Ingredients:

1 package dry yeast
2 cups warm water
3 tbsps. sugar or honey
4 cups whole wheat flour
1 tsp. oil
1 tsp. salt

Preparation:

Mix yeast, warm water and sugar in a small bowl and let rise for 5 minutes or until bubbly. In a large bowl mix other ingredients, add yeast mixture and knead dough on a lightly floured surface for 6 or 8 minutes. Make a soft dough that is smooth and elastic, place dough in an oiled bowl, cover and set in a warm place to rise. Let rise until double in size, pinch down and let rise for 15 minutes. Roll out and shape in large or small loaves. Place in a nonstick or greased baking pan and let rise until double in size. Bake in an oven at 350 degrees for 45 minutes or until golden brown.

MACARONI PIE

Ingredients:

1 lb. elbow macaroni
1 cup milk
1 lb. package of cheese, grated
1 egg
2 tsps. butter
2 tsps. salt
6 cups water
1 tsp. onion powder
1/4 tsp. garlic powder

Preparation:

Pour water in a pot, bring to a boil, add macaroni, cook and drain off water. Pour in a bowl, add 1/4 cup cheese and all other ingredients and mix. Pour into a greased baking dish, sprinkle bread crumbs and cheese on top and bake in oven at 350 degrees for 30 minutes or until brown.

LASAGNA

Ingredients:

1 lb. package lasagna pasta, cooked
1 28-ounce jar spaghetti sauce
1 lb. ground beef or turkey
1lb. package Monterey Jack cheese
1 tsp. garlic powder
2 tsps. Lawry's seasoning salt
1 tsp. paprika
1 tsp. onion powder

Preparation:

In a pot pour spaghetti sauce, add beef and other seasonings, and cook for 20 minutes. In a greased pie dish lay pasta side by side, pour meat mixture on top of pasta and make another layer of pasta and meat. Repeat layer with remaining pasta and meat mixture. Make three layers. Sprinkle remaining cheese on top, cover with a piece of foil and bake in an oven at 350 degrees for 40 minutes.

STEAMED CABBAGE

Ingredients:

1 medium cabbage, chopped
1 medium onion, sliced into strips
1 tbsp. Lawry's seasoning salt
2 tsp. oil
3/4 cup water

Preparation:

Pour water in a pot, bring to a boil and add cabbage, onions and seasoning. Stir, cover, reduce heat and simmer until done.

SCRAMBLED TOFU

Ingredients:

1 lb. tofu
1/4 cup onions, chopped
1/4 cup red sweet peppers, chopped
1/4 cup green sweet peppers, chopped
2 garlic cloves, chopped
1 tbsp. soy sauce
1 tbsp. Lawry's seasoning salt
1/3 tsp. turmeric
1 tbsp. oil

Preparation:

Rinse tofu, drain and scramble. In a skillet simmer vegetables with oil, add tofu and seasonings and heat thoroughly.

SCALLOPED POTATOES

Ingredients:

6 medium potatoes
1 1/2 cups milk or water
1 cup cheese, grated
2 cloves garlic, minced
1 small onion, chopped
1 tsp. oil
2 tbsps. Lawry seasoning salt
2 tsps. flour

Preparation:

In a sauce pan simmer onions and garlic in oil. Stir in flour and seasoning, add milk, bring to a boil and heat until thickened. Peel potatoes, wash and cut lengthwise or round in thin slices. Place potato slices in a baking dish, pour cream mixture over potatoes, cover with a piece of foil and bake in an oven at 350 degrees for 40 minutes or until tender. Remove from oven, uncover and sprinkle with cheese. Bake for 5 minutes more uncovered.

CARROT CAKE

Ingredients:

2 cups flour, sifted
3/4 cup milk
1/4 cup sugar
1/2 cup raisins
1/4 cup nuts, chopped
1 cup carrots, peeled and grated
1 tsp. vanilla essence
1/4 cup oil
Pinch of salt
1 tbsp. baking powder

Preparation:

In large bowl mix flour, baking powder and salt. Add raisins, nuts, vanilla and carrots. Whisk oil, sugar and milk in a small bowl. Pour into large bowl and mix until flour is moistened. Pour mixture in a greased baking pan and bake in an oven at 350 degrees for 25 minutes. Insert a toothpick in center of cake and remove. If toothpick comes out clean the cake is done.

RED KIDNEY BEANS SOUP

Ingredients:

3 cups red kidney beans
2 cups carrots, sliced
2 cups potatoes, cut into cubes
10 cups water
1 lb. beef
1/2 cup onions, chopped
1/2 cup red sweet peppers, chopped
1 cup coconut milk
2 cloves garlic, minced
1 tbsp. Lawry's seasoning salt
1 tsp. black pepper
1 tsp. butter
3 sprigs fresh thyme
Salt to taste

Preparation:

Wash meat, cut into small pieces and add seasonings. Pour water in a large pot and add meat and kidney beans. Cook for 20 minutes. When cooked, add all other ingredients and cook for 30 minutes.

PUMPKIN PIE

Ingredients:

2 1/2 cups pumpkin, cooked and mashed
1/2 cup sugar
1 cup milk
1 tbsp. cinnamon
1/2 tsp. nutmeg
3 eggs
1 tbsp. vanilla essence
2 tbsps. butter
1/2 tsp. salt
1/4 cup arrowroot starch or corn starch

Preparation:

Wash and cut pumpkin. Cook in a pot with water and when cooked scrape pumpkin from the skin. Place pumpkin in a bowl and mash. Add all ingredients and mix until smooth. Pour into a pie crust and bake in an oven at 350 degrees for 50 minutes or until brown.

PELAU

Ingredients:

2 cups rice
1 lb. beef or chicken
1/2 lb. lentils
1 1/2 tsps. sugar
1 tbsp. butter
1 tbsp. tomato paste
1 tsp. oil
1/2 cup onions, chopped
1/2 cup green sweet peppers, chopped
1/2 cup red sweet peppers, chopped
1 tsp. black pepper
2 cloves of garlic, minced
8 cups water

Preparation:

Wash meat and cut into small pieces. Add seasonings. In a hot pot add oil and sugar to brown. Do not brown too dark or use dark coloring. Add meat and let it brown in coloring. Add a little water and stir. When meat is colored, add peppers, onions and garlic and simmer. Pour in water to cook meat. When meat is tender add lentils and cook for 5 minutes. Wash rice, add to pot, add other ingredients and cook until done..

BREADFRUIT SALAD

Ingredients:

1/2 of a breadfruit
1 tsp. yellow mustard
1 cup mayonnaise
1/4 cup onions, finely chopped
1/4 cup red sweet peppers, diced
1 tsp. garlic powder or garlic minced
1/4 tsp. salt

Preparation:

Peel, wash, and cut breadfruit into 1 inch pieces. Cook in a pot with water until tender. Place breadfruit in a bowl, add all ingredients, mix, chill and serve.

OATMEAL

Ingredients:

2 cups quick oatmeal
3 1/2 cups milk
2 tbsps. sugar or honey
1 tsp. cinnamon
1 medium banana, sliced

Preparation:

In a pot pour milk and cinnamon. Bring to a boil, add oatmeal and sugar, stir and cook for 2 minutes. Serve with bananas.

PEANUT BUTTER COOKIES

Ingredients:

1/2 cup peanut butter, crunchy
1/4 cup sugar
1 cup flour
1/4 cup raisins
1/4 cup water
1 tsp. vanilla essence
1/4 tsp. salt

Preparation:

In a bowl mix peanut butter, sugar, vanilla and other ingredients. Form dough into cookies using a fork to flatten. Bake on a greased shallow pan in oven at 350 degrees for 20 minutes.

DUCANA

Ingredients:

6 sweet potatoes, grated
1 cup coconut, grated
1/2 cup sugar
1 tsp. ginger, grated
1 tsp. cinnamon
1/2 tsp. salt
1/2 cup flour or large tannia grated
1 tsp. vanilla essence
Banana leaves

Preparation:

Peel, wash and grate potatoes and coconut in a large bowl. Add other ingredients and mix. Warm banana leaves over the stove, pour some of the mixture into a piece of banana leaf, fold and tie with a piece of string or use aluminum foil. Make as much as you want and cook in a large pot with boiling water for 20 minutes or until done. When cool unwrap and serve.

MASHED POTATOES

Ingredients:

2 lbs. of potatoes
1/2 cup milk
1 tbsp. butter
1 tbsp. Lawry's seasoning salt
1/2 tsp. garlic powder
1/2 tsp. onion powder
1/4 tsp. salt

Preparation:

Peel, wash and cook potatoes in a pot with small amount of water. When cooked place in a bowl, add ingredients and mash..

BANANA MUFFINS

Ingredients:

3 bananas (ripe and smashed chunky)
2 cups flour
1/2 cup sugar
1 tsp. vanilla
1/4 cup oil
1 cup warm water or milk
1 tbsp. dry active yeast
1/2 tsp. salt

Preparation:

Mix warm water and yeast in a small bowl and set aside. Blend oil and sugar in a large bowl and add bananas, vanilla, flour, salt and yeast. Mix together. Pour into a greased muffin pan, let rise for 10 minutes, and bake in oven at 350 degrees for 15 minutes or until brown.

SWEET POTATO COBBLER

Ingredients:

2 lbs. potatoes
1/2 cup brown sugar or honey
1 tsp. vanilla essence
2 tbsps. butter
6 cups water

Preparation:

Peel, wash and cut potatoes in round slices. Pour water in a pot, bring to a boil, add potatoes and cook for 5 minutes. Remove and place in a baking dish, mix sugar or honey, vanilla and melted butter, and pour on top of potatoes. Bake in oven at 350 degrees for 20 minutes or until lightly brown.

POTATO FRIES

Ingredients:

2 large potatoes
1 tbsp. Lawry's seasoning salt

Preparation:

Peel and wash potatoes. Slice lengthwise, 1/2 inch thick, and cut into French fry strips. Place in a greased baking pan, sprinkle seasoning on potatoes, and salt to taste. Bake in oven at 400 degrees for 30 minutes or until tender and brown.

BARBEQUE SAUCE

Ingredients:

1 cup tomato sauce
1/4 cup tomato paste
1 tsp. onion powder
1 tbsp. garlic powder
1/4 cup lemon juice
3 tbsps. molasses
2 tbsps. soy sauce
3 tbsps. sugar or honey
1/2 tsp. salt

Preparation:

Place all ingredients in a pot and bring to a boil. Reduce heat and simmer uncovered for 20 minutes.

WHITE BREAD

Ingredients:

1 package dry active yeast
1/4 cup warm water
2 cups hot milk
2 tbsps. sugar
6 cups flour, sifted
1 tbsp. butter
1 tbsp. salt
1 tsp. oil

Preparation:

In a small bowl mix yeast and sugar in warm water. Let rise for 5 minutes or until bubbly. In a large bowl pour milk and add shortening and salt. Stir in 2 cups flour, mix well and add remaining flour. Pour in yeast mixture and mix to make a stiff dough. Place dough on a lightly floured surface and knead until smooth and elastic.

Place in oiled bowl, cover and set in a warm place to rise. Let rise until double in size. Pinch down, let rise for 15 minutes and shape into loaves. Place in a greased baking pan, let rise until double in size, and bake in oven at 350 degrees for 45 minutes or until golden brown.

RICE AND PEAS

Ingredients:

1 15 oz. can dry pigeon peas, rinsed and drained
2 cups rice
6 cups water
2 cloves of garlic, minced
1/4 cup onions, chopped
1 tsp. salt

Preparation:

In a large pot bring water to a boil and add onions, salt and garlic. Wash rice and add to pot. When rice is tender add peas, stir, lower heat and cook for 5 or 10 minutes.

STEWED BEEF

Ingredients:

1 lb. beef
4 cups water
1/2 cup onions, chopped
1/2 cup green sweet peppers, chopped
1/2 cup red sweet peppers, chopped
1 tsp. black pepper
2 cloves of garlic, minced
1 tbsp. Lawry's seasoning salt
1 tsp. salt
1 1/2 tbsps. sugar
1 tsp. oil
1 tsp. tomato paste
1 cup carrots, diced

Preparation:

Wash and cut beef in small pieces and add seasonings. In a medium hot pot add oil and sugar to brown. Do not brown to dark or use dark coloring. Add meat and let it brown in coloring. Add a little water and stir. When meat is brown add onions, peppers and garlic. Add water and simmer to cook meat. When meat is tender add carrots, tomato paste and salt to taste. Cook for 10 minutes. Serve with rice and peas.